First published in the United States in 1991 by
Gallery Books, an imprint of W.H. Smith Publishers, Inc.,
112 Madison Avenue, New York, New York 10016
Copyright © 1986 by The Five Mile Press.
Illustrated by Bob Graham.
Produced by Joshua Morris Publishing, Inc.
in association with The Five Mile Press.
All rights reserved.
Printed in Singapore.
ISBN 0-8317-0930-8

Gallery Books are available for bulk purchase
for sales promotions and premium use. For
details write or telephone the Manager of
Special Sales, W.H. Smith Publishers, Inc.,
112 Madison Avenue, New York, New York 10016,
212 ... 600

It's Much Too Hot!

An early learner book about heat

bob graham

GALLERY BOOKS
An Imprint of W. H. Smith Publishers Inc.
112 Madison Avenue
New York City 10016

It's much too hot.
Look at the flowers.

It's too hot for dogs.
Look at Patch's tongue.

And it's too hot for Jenny.
Look at her mop her wet brow.

There is only one place for Patch.

It's cooler in the shade of a tree.

Jenny's feet are hot and sticky.
Look how pink they are.

There is only one thing to
do with feet like that.

There is only one thing to
do with the hose.

Jenny feels much cooler.

Her droopy flowers may soon
feel better too.

When Jenny stops hosing,
the heat will dry the puddles.

Jenny is looking for things to hose.
Patch will find another cool shadow.

He does not like water games.

When the sun goes down…

…it will be much cooler.

heat

When a liquid becomes a vapor, the heat which caused the change is known as the *latent heat of evaporation*. When evaporation occurs, the water seems to disappear into the air—however this is not the case. All matter consists of tiny particles. In liquids these molecules are widely separated, but in gases they are even further apart. When heated, molecules move about rapidly and get further part until they eventually escape as vapor.

Experiments to try
1. On a hot day, children can put their hands on a hot sidewalk and watch their impressions evaporate.
2. Puddles provide a good example of evaporation—outline a puddle in chalk and after, say, 10 minutes make another outline and note how much has evaporated.
3. Place a mixture of water and salt in a saucer and leave it in a sunny place. What is left when the water evaporates?
4. Time how long it takes for an ice block to melt.
   a. In the sun
   b. In the shade